Talk To Me In Korean
Workbook
Level 3

written & designed by
Talk To Me In Korean

Talk To Me In Korean Workbook (Level 3)

1판 1쇄 · 1st edition published	2014. 1. 2.
1판 17쇄 · 17th edition published	2024. 2. 12.

지은이 · Written by	Talk To Me In Korean
책임편집 · Edited by	선경화 Kyung-hwa Sun, 스테파니 베이츠 Stephanie Bates
디자인 · Designed by	선윤아 Yoona Sun
삽화 · Illustrations by	장성원 Kanari Jones
녹음 · Voice Recordings by	선경화 Kyung-hwa Sun
펴낸곳 · Published by	롱테일북스 Longtail Books
펴낸이 · Publisher	이수영 Su Young Lee
편집 · Copy-edited by	김보경 Florence Kim
주소 · Address	04033 서울특별시 마포구 양화로 113, 3층(서교동, 순흥빌딩)
	3rd Floor, 113 Yanghwa-ro, Mapo-gu, Seoul, KOREA
이메일 · E-mail	TTMIK@longtailbooks.co.kr
ISBN	978-89-5605-690-6 14710

*이 교재의 내용을 사전 허가 없이 전재하거나 복제할 경우 법적인 제재를 받게 됨을 알려 드립니다.

*잘못된 책은 구입하신 서점이나 본사에서 교환해 드립니다.

*정가는 표지에 표시되어 있습니다.

TTMIK - TALK TO ME IN KOREAN

Talk To Me
In Korean
Workbook
Level 3

Contents

How to Use the Talk To Me In Korean Workbook

This workbook is designed to be used in conjunction with the Talk To Me In Korean Level 3 lessons, which are available as both a paperback book and an online course at https://talktomeinkorean.com. Developed by certified teachers to help you review and reinforce what you've learned in the Talk To Me In Korean lessons, this workbook contains 3 main categories of review and 16 types of exercises:

Categories

1. Vocabulary
2. Comprehension
3. Dictation

Types of Exercises

1. Writing
2. Reading
3. Matching
4. Complete the dialogue
5. Fill in the blank
6. Complete the sentence
7. Multiple choice
8. Translation
   (Korean <-> English)
9. Short answer
10. Define and translate

11. Fill in the conjugation chart

12. True/False

13. Q&A

14. Vocabulary builder pyramid

15. Situational expressions

16. Vocabulary web

The "Dictation" category is designed to aid in the development of Korean listening skills. You simply listen to the corresponding audio file and write down what you hear. In order to benefit the most from this category, it is important that you download the available audio files from https://talktomeinkorean.com/audio or access them through our audio mobile application, TTMIK: Audio.

We encourage you to learn how to read and write 한글 if you do not know how to do so already. Although romanizations were provided in the Level 1 and Level 2 workbooks, they will not be provided in any workbooks from Level 3 onward. Please refer to our "Quick Guide to 한글" in this book if you need assistance in reading or writing 한글.

Quick Guide To 한글 (Hangeul)

The Korean alphabet is called 한글 (Hangeul), and there are 24 basic letters and digraphs in 한글.

*digraph: pair of characters used to make one sound (phoneme)

Of the letters, fourteen are consonants (자음), and five of them are doubled to form the five tense consonants (쌍자음).

Consonants

Basic

ㄱ	ㄴ	ㄷ	ㄹ	ㅁ	ㅂ	ㅅ	ㅇ	ㅈ	ㅊ	ㅋ	ㅌ	ㅍ	ㅎ
g/k	n	d/t	r/l	m	b/p	s	ng	j	ch	k	t	p	h
g/k	n	d/t	r/l	m	b/p	s/ɕ	ŋ	dʑ/tɕ	tɕʰ	k/kʰ	t/tʰ	p/pʰ	h

Tense

ㄲ	ㄸ		ㅃ	ㅆ		ㅉ
kk	tt		pp	ss		jj
k'	t'		p'	s'		c'

The pronunciations of each consonant above, however, apply when the consonant is used as a beginning consonant. When those consonants are used as the final consonant of a syllable block, only seven consonants are pronounced; ㄱ, ㄴ, ㄷ, ㄹ, ㅁ, ㅂ, and ㅇ. The rest of the consonants are pronounced as one of these seven consonants when they are used as a final consonant.

* ㅋ and ㄲ are pronounced as ㄱ when they are used as a final consonant.

* ㅅ, ㅈ, ㅊ, ㅌ, ㅎ, and ㅆ are pronounced as ㄷ when they are used as a final consonant.

* ㅍ is pronounced as ㅂ when used as a final consonant.

* ㄸ, ㅃ, and ㅉ are not used as a final consonant.

When it comes to vowels (모음), there are 10 basic letters. 11 additional letters can be created by combining certain basic letters to make a total of 21 vowels. Of the vowels, eight are single pure vowels, also known as monophthongs (단모음), and 13 are diphthongs (이중모음), or two vowel sounds joined into one syllable which creates one sound.

*When saying a monophthong, you are producing one pure vowel with no tongue movement.
*When saying a diphthong, you are producing one sound by saying two vowels. Therefore, your tongue and mouth move quickly from one letter to another (glide or slide) to create a single sound.

Vowels

Monophthongs

ㅏ	ㅓ	ㅗ	ㅜ	ㅡ	ㅣ	ㅐ	ㅔ
a	eo	o	u	eu	i	ae	e
a/aː	ʌ/əː	o/oː	u/uː	ɨ/ɯː	i/iː	ɛ/ɛː	e/eː

Diphthongs

ㅑ	ㅕ	ㅛ	ㅠ		ㅒ	ㅖ	
ya	yeo	yo	yu		yae	ye	
ja	jʌ	jo	ju		jɛ	je	
ㅘ	ㅝ				ㅙ	ㅞ	
wa	wo				wae	we	
wa	wʌ/wəː				wɛ	we	
					ㅚ	ㅟ	ㅢ
					oe	wi	ui
					we	wi	ɨi

* ㅚ and ㅟ were pronounced as single pure vowels (monophthongs) in the past; however, presently, these vowels are produced as two vowels gradually gliding into one another to create one sound (diphthong).
* Please refer to the book "한글마스터(Hangeul Master)" for more information.

Writing 한글 letters

한글 is written top to bottom, left to right. For example:

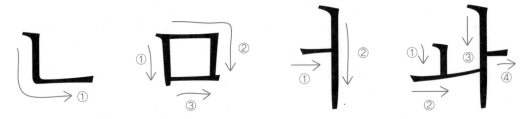

By making sure you follow the stroke order rules, you will find that writing Korean is quite easy and other people will be able to better read your handwriting.

Syllable Blocks

Each Korean syllable is written in a way that forms a block-like shape, with each letter inside the block forming a sound/syllable.

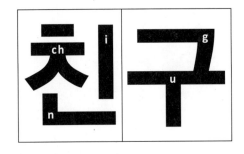

In each syllable block, there is a:

1. * Beginning consonant

2. * Middle vowel

3. Optional final consonant

* Required in a syllable block. A block MUST contain a minimum of two letters: 1 consonant and 1 vowel.

ㅊ + ㅣ + ㄴ (ch+i+n) = chin

ㄱ + ㅜ (g+u) = gu

친 (chin) + 구 (gu) = 친구 (chingu) = "friend"

Two of the most common ways to write consonant and vowel combinations in Korean are horizontally and vertically (the boxes drawn here are for illustrative purpose only).

C *Consonant*   **V** *Vowel*

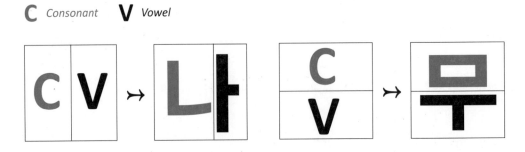

Talk To Me In Korean Workbook

By adding a final consonant (받침), the blocks are modified:

C *Consonant*   **V** *Vowel*

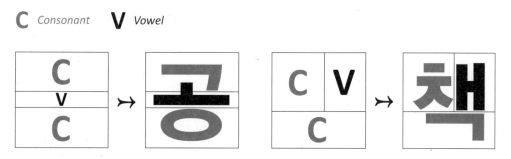

There are also syllables which have two final consonants, such as:

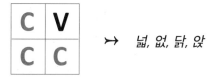

→   넓, 없, 닭, 앉

In all the syllable blocks, the letters are either compressed or stretched to keep the size relatively the same as the other letters.

Place Holder In Front Of Vowels

Since the "minimum two letter" rule exists and one letter has to be a consonant and the other has to be a vowel, what can you do when a vowel needs to be written in its own syllable block? Add the consonant ㅇ [ng] in front of or on top of the vowel. When reading a vowel, such as 아, the ㅇ makes no sound and you just pronounce the ㅏ [a].

Vowels absolutely, cannot, under any circumstances be written by themselves!!

Okay! Now that you are equipped with a basic knowledge of 한글,

it's time to do your part and start practicing!

Let's get to it!

Lesson 1.
Too much, very   너무

Section I – Vocabulary

Please define/translate each word to English. Then write it in your preferred language (if not English).

1. 비싸다 _____

2. 크다 _____

3. 시끄럽다 _____

4. 덥다 _____

5. 빠르다 _____

6. 어렵다 _____

7. 슬프다 _____

8. 쉽다 _____

9. 쓰다 (adj) _____

10. 짜다 _____

11. 맵다 _____

12. 맛있다 _____

Section II - Writing practice

Using the adjectives from Section I and the adverb 너무, write a statement in 존댓말, then translate the statement to English and your preferred language (if not English).

Example: (given) 아름답다
"너무 아름다워요." = It's very beautiful.

1a: _____

2a: _____

3a: _____

4a: _____

5a: _____

6a: _____

7a: _____

8a: _____

9a: _____

10a: _____

11a: _____

12a: _____

Section III - Dictation

Listen to the corresponding MP3 file. Repeat what you hear out loud, then write it down. Each word/phrase will be said twice.

13. Track 1:

14. Track 2_ver2:

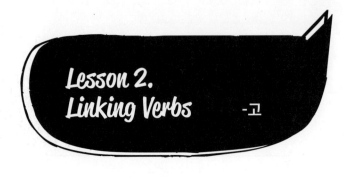

Lesson 2.
Linking Verbs -고

Section I - Vocabulary

Match each Korean word to its common English translation.

1.	영화	a.	friend
2.	서점	b.	movie
3.	운동	c.	to be cheap
4.	9월	d.	bookstore
5.	일본	e.	stomach
6.	배부르다	f.	exercise
7.	도너츠	g.	donut
8.	배	h.	September
9.	친구	i.	to be full
10.	싸다	j.	Japan

Section II – Comprehension

Answer the following questions in English and your preferred language (if not English).

11. Explain what -고 does.

12. What makes -고 different from the English conjunction "and"?

13. Why does using -고 work when you are talking about things that happened in a sequence?

Section III - Writing practice

Connect the sentences by using -고 and rewrite each sentence on the given line.

   Example:

   내일 쇼핑몰에 갈 거예요. 서점에 갈 거예요.

   ↳ 내일 쇼핑몰에 가고, 서점에 갈 거예요.

14. 10월에는 일본에 갈 거예요. 11월에는 미국에 갈 거예요.

15. 오늘은 커피숍에서 친구를 만났어요. 한국어 공부했어요.

_____

16. 삼겹살 먹었어요. 김치 먹었어요. 마늘 먹었어요. 고추 먹었어요. 밥 먹었어요.
지금 배가 너무 불러요.

_____

17. 수영했어요. 영어 공부했어요. 점심 먹었어요.

_____

Section IV - Dictation

Listen to the corresponding MP3 file. Repeat what you hear
out loud, then write it down. Each word/phrase will be said
twice.

18. Track 3:

19. Track 4:

Lesson 3.   앞에, 뒤에, 위에, 밑에, 옆에
In front of, behind, on top of,
under, next to

Section I - Vocabulary

Choose the image which best represents the Korean postposition.

1. 뒤에   a.

2. 앞에   b.

3. 위에   c.

4. 밑에   d.

5. 옆에   e.

Section II - Complete the dialogue

Choose the word which best completes each dialogue.
Not all words are used, and some of the words can
be used more than once.

--- Word Bank ---

뒤에   위에   옆에

앞에   밑에

6.

경화: 우리 어디에서 만날 거예요? = *Where are we going to meet?*

효진: 은행 _____ 서요. = *In front of the bank.*

경화: 왜요? 카페에서 안 만날 거예요? = *Why? We are not going to meet at the cafe?*

7.

재석: 저 강아지 보여요? = *Do you see that dog?*

광수: 어디요? = *Where?*

재석: 저기요. 자동차 _____ 있어요. = *Over there. It's on top of the car.*

광수: 안 보여요. = *I can't see it.*

재석: 아, 지금은 차 _____ 있어요. = *Oh, now it's under the car.*

8.

경은: 반지를 잃어버렸어요. = I've lost my ring.

현정: 소파 _____ 보세요. = Look under the couch.

경은: 소파 _____ 없었어요. = It wasn't under the couch.

현정: 소파 _____ 도 보세요. = Look behind the couch as well.

Section III - Dictation
Listen to the corresponding MP3 file. Repeat what you hear out loud, then fill in the blanks with the missing word. Each phrase will be said twice.

9. Track 5: 은행은 학교 _____ 있어요.

10. Track 6: 강아지는 자동차 _____ 있어요.

11. Track 7: 컴퓨터는 책상 _____ 있어요.

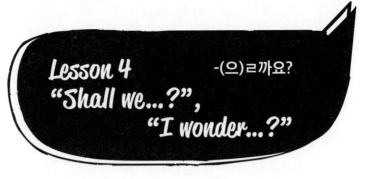

Lesson 4
"Shall we...?",
"I wonder...?"

-(으)ㄹ까요?

Section I - Comprehension

True/False – Decide if the statement is true or false. If it is false, correct the underlined term or statement so that the sentence is true.

1. You can use the ending -(으)ㄹ까요? when you want to <u>invite others to do something with you and ask "shall we do this together?"</u> and when you ask yourself or others "I wonder what it is?"

   ≫

2. When using -(으)ㄹ까요? in the past tense, you can <u>add the past tense suffix -았/었/였 right after the verb stem and before -(으)ㄹ까요?</u> to make an assumption about a past event.

   ≫

3. If a verb stem ends in a vowel, such as 오다, when conjugated with -(으)ㄹ까요?, it becomes <u>오을까요?</u>

   ≫

Section II - Vocabulary and Conjugation

Verb (infinitive form)	English definition	+ -(으)ㄹ까요?
ex. 하다	to do	할까요?
4. 마시다		
5. 시작하다		
6. 놓다		
7. 달리다		
8. 만들다		
9. 앉다		

Section III - Complete the sentence

Complete the sentence by conjugating the given verb with the -(으)ㄹ까요 ending. Then translate each sentence to English and your preferred language (if not English) on the given line.

10. 책을 어디에 _____? (놓다)

= _____

11. 언제 다시 _____? (전화하다)

= _____

12. 산에 _____? (가다)

= _____

13. 내일 비가 _____? (오다)

= _____

14. 여기에서 사진 _____? (찍다)

= _____

Section IV - Dictation

Listen to the corresponding MP3 file. Repeat what you hear out loud, then write it down. Each word/phrase will be said twice.

15. Track 8:

16. Track 9:

17. Track 10_ver2:

Lesson 5
Approximately, about
쯤, 정도, 약

Section I - Vocabulary and Comprehension
Circle the best answer.

1. The Korean word for "Germany" is:

    a. 한국

    b. 미국

    c. 영국

    d. 독일

2. What is the Korean counter used for animals?

    a. 명

    b. 병

    c. 마리

    d. 개

3. When telling time in Korean, how do you count the hours?

    a. with Sino-Korean numbers (일, 이, 삼...) + 시

    b. with Sino Korean numbers + 분

    c. with Native Korean numbers (하나, 둘, 셋...) + 시

    d. with Native Korean numbers + 분

4. "2월" translates to English as:

    a. January

    b. February

    c. March

    d. April

5. Written in 한글, 6,000 won is:

    a. 천 원

    b. 백 원

    c. 오백 원

    d. 육천 원

6. 쯤 means:

    a. near

    b. on top

    c. approximately, about

    d. 4 o'clock

7. -(으)ㄹ 거예요 is used when forming what verb tense?

    a. future tense

    b. past tense

    c. present tense

    d. past progressive tense

8. Where is 쯤 placed in a sentence?

    a. before nouns

    b. before verbs

    c. after nouns

    d. after verbs

9. What is the most common way to say "approximately" or "about" in Korean?

    a. 약

    b. 정도

    c. 킬로미터

    d. 쯤

10. Which two Korean words are sometimes used together to express "approximately" or "about"?

    a. 약 and 정도

    b. 쯤 and 정도

    c. 약 and 쯤

    d. both A and C

    e. both A and B

    f. none of these

11. The word "약" can mean "approximately" or "about", but also " _____ " depending on the context.

    a. medicine   c. example

    b. cup   d. yarn

Section II - Complete the dialogue

Using the word 쯤 and the prompts in parenthesis, complete each dialogue in Korean.

12. A: 도서관에 학생이 몇 명 있어요?

    B: ﹏﹏﹏﹏﹏﹏﹏﹏﹏﹏﹏﹏﹏﹏ .
    (about 100 people)

13. A: 지금 현금 얼마 있어요? * 현금 = cash

    B: ﹏﹏﹏﹏﹏﹏﹏﹏﹏﹏﹏﹏﹏ .
    (about 20,000 won)

14. A: ﹏﹏﹏﹏﹏﹏﹏﹏﹏﹏﹏﹏﹏ ?
    (About what time are you going to go?)

    B: 두 시쯤 갈 거예요.

15. A: ﹏﹏﹏﹏﹏﹏﹏﹏﹏﹏﹏﹏﹏ ?
    (Around what time shall we meet tomorrow?)

    B: 일곱 시쯤 만날까요?

Section III - Dictation

Listen to the corresponding MP3 file. Repeat what you hear out loud, then write it down. Each word/phrase will be said twice.

16. Track 11:

17. Track 12:

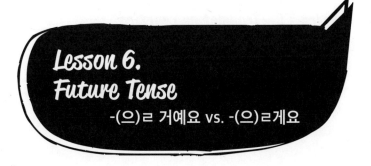

Lesson 6.
Future Tense
-(으)ㄹ 거예요 vs. -(으)ㄹ게요

Section I - Comprehension

Answer the following questions in English and your preferred language (if not English).

1. What is the main difference between -(으)ㄹ 거예요 and -(으)ㄹ게요?

   >>

2. List the 3 situations in which you can use -(으)ㄹ게요 instead of -(으)ㄹ 거예요:

   a.

   b.

   c.

Section II - Translation practice

Translate the following sentences to Korean using either -(으)ㄹ 거예요 or -(으)ㄹ게요.

3. I am going to the park (no matter what you say).

    =

4. (If you don't mind) I will come along, too.

    =

5. I will call you tomorrow (for your sake/because of what you said).

    =

6. Kyung-hwa is going out (no matter what).

    =

7. I will go out now (unless you don't want me to).

    =

Section III - Reading Comprehension

Underline the correct or most likely answer. If both answers are possible, underline both items.

8. A: 내일 뭐 (할 거예요 / 할게요)?

    B: 친구 생일 파티에 (갈 거예요 / 갈게요).

9. A: 이 책 (줄 거예요 / 줄게요).
    (You are handing the person the book as you say this.)

    B: 저한테요? 감사합니다.

10. A: 저는 내년에 한국어 (공부할 거예요 / 공부할게요). * 내년 = next year

    B: 그래요? 제가 (도와줄 거예요 / 도와줄게요).

Section IV - Dictation

Listen to the corresponding MP3 file. Repeat what you hear out loud, then write it down. Each word/phrase will be said twice.

11. Track 13:

12. Track 14:

13. Track 15:

Lesson 7.
Linking Verbs -아/어/여서

Section I - Comprehension

Complete the sentences by using the words in the box + -아/어/여서. Then translate each sentence to English and your preferred language (if not English).

먹다	공부하다	오다
가다	모으다	아프다

1. 지민 씨는 _____ 집에 갔어요. =

2. 돈 _____ 뭐 할 거예요? =

3. 집에 빨리 _____ 쉬고 싶어요. =

4. 너무 많이 _____ 배불러요. =

5. 열심히 _____ 장학금 받을 거예요. =

6. 여기 _____ 이거 보세요. =

Section II - Writing practice

Connect the sentences by using -아/어/여서 and rewrite each sentence on the given line.

Example:

비가 와요. 못 가요. ➜ <u>비가 와서 못 가요.</u>

7. 오늘은 바빠요. 영화를 못 봐요.

_____

8. 공원에 갈 거예요. 책을 읽을 거예요.

_____

9. 친구를 만났어요. 밥을 먹었어요.

_____

10. 케이크를 살 거예요. 친구한테 줄 거예요.

_____

Section III - Translation practice

Translate the following sentences to Korean
using -아/어/여서 structure.

11. After you go to Korea, what are you going to do?

     =

12. I'm glad to have come to Seoul.

     =

13. It rained, so I stayed at home.

     =

14. These days I'm busy, so I can't meet my friends.

     =

Section IV - Dictation

Listen to the corresponding MP3 file. Repeat what you hear
out loud, then write it down. Each word/phrase will be said
twice.

15. Track 16_ver2:

16. Track 17:

Lesson 8.
To look like, to seem like
(used with nouns)
-같아요

Section I - Vocabulary

Match each English word to its common Korean equivalent.

1. Tokyo

2. Seoul

3. Korean melon

4. robot

5. angel

6. genius

7. lie

8. puppy

9. cat

10. age

a. 거짓말

b. 나이

c. 강아지

d. 로봇

e. 고양이

f. 서울

g. 참외

h. 천사

i. 천재

j. 도쿄

Section II - Translation Practice

Translate the following sentences to English and your preferred language (if not English).

11. 현우 씨는 로봇 같아요.

     =

12. 비올라는 바이올린하고 비슷해요.

     =

13. 효진 씨는 천재 같아요.

     =

14. 이 가방하고 저 가방은 같아요.

     =

Section III - Reading comprehension

Read the following journal entry. Unless otherwise noted, all words, sentence endings, and tenses have been covered in TTMIK Levels 1-3. Based on what you read, answer the questions below in Korean.

* 도착하다 = to arrive
* 따뜻하다 = to be warm

오늘 서울에 도착했어요. 서울 날씨는 도쿄 날씨하고 비슷해요. 그렇지만 서울이 도쿄보다 조금 더 추워요. 그래서 옷을 따뜻하게 입었어요. 저녁에는 효진 씨를 만나서 같이 밥을 먹었어요. 효진 씨는 저랑 나이가 같아요. 그렇지만 서로 존댓말로 말해요.

15. Where is the writer?

16. What place has weather similar to Seoul?

17. Where is it colder, Seoul or Tokyo?

18. Who did the writer meet today?

19. What did the writer do with Hyojin?

20. What do Hyojin and the writer have in common?

Section IV - Dictation
Listen to the corresponding MP3 file. Repeat what you hear out loud, then write it down. Each word/phrase will be said twice.

21. Track 18:

22. Track 19:

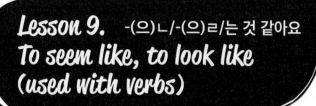

Lesson 9. -(으)ㄴ/-(으)ㄹ/는 것 같아요
To seem like, to look like
(used with verbs)

Section I - Vocabulary

Translate each word to English, then write it in your preferred language (if not English).

1. 이야기하다 =

2. 비싸다 =

3. 그렇다 =

4. 멀다 =

5. 예쁘다 =

6. 눈 =

7. 이상하다 =

Section II - Conjugation chart

Fill in the chart by writing the meaning for the given verb/phrase, then conjugate it with the given sentence endings.

Verb/Phrase (infinitive)	Meaning	+ -(으)ㄴ 것 같아요	+ -는 것 같아요	+ -(으)ㄹ 것 같아요
8. 말하다				
9. 일어나다				
10. 자다				
11. 공부하다				
12. 사다				
13. 연습하다				
14. 숙제를 하다				
15. 돈을 모으다				
16. 눈이 오다				

Section III - Comprehension

Choose the most suitable word or phrase to complete the dialogue.

17. A: 이 청바지 예뻐요?

    B: 네. 그런데 조금 ～～～～～～～～～～～～～ .

        a. 작인 것 같아요   c. 작는 것 같아요

        b. 작은 것 같아요   d. 잘은 것 같아요

18. A: 이 참외 진짜 맛있어요!

    B: 그렇지만 너무 ～～～～～～～～～～～～～ .

        a. 비쌌 것 같아요   c. 비싼 것 같아요

        b. 쌀 것 같아요   d. 비싸는 것 같아요

19. A: 석진 씨 어디 갔어요?

    B: 벌써 집에 ～～～～～～～～～～～～～ .

        a. 가는 것 같아요   c. 갔 것 같아요

        b. 갈 것 같아요   d. 간 것 같아요

20. A: 저 케이크 보세요. ～～～～～～～～～～～～～ .

    B: 저거 살까요?

        a. 맛있은 것 같아요   c. 맛있을 것 같아요

        b. 맛있는 것 같아요   d. 맛있었 것 같아요

21. A: 이 영화 볼까요?

　　B: 그 영화 별로 ＿＿＿＿＿＿＿＿＿＿＿＿＿＿.

　　　　a. 재밌는 것 같아요　　　c. 재미없는 것 같아요

　　　　b. 재밌을 것 같아요　　　d. 재미없을 것 같아요

22. A: 주원 씨가 학교 선생님이에요?

　　B: 네. 영어 ＿＿＿＿＿＿＿＿＿＿＿＿＿＿.

　　　　a. 선생님인 것 같아요　　　c. 선생님는 것 같아요

　　　　b. 선생님 것 같아요　　　d. 선생님이는 것 같아요

Section IV - Dictation

Listen to the corresponding MP3 file. Repeat what you hear out loud, then fill in the blanks with the missing word. Each phrase will be said twice.

23. Track 20: 혜미 씨는 ＿＿＿＿＿＿＿＿＿＿＿＿＿＿＿＿＿＿＿.

24. Track 21: 그 사람은 요즘 ＿＿＿＿＿＿＿＿＿＿＿＿＿＿＿.

25. Track 22: 그것도 ＿＿＿＿＿＿＿＿＿＿＿＿＿＿＿＿＿＿.

Lesson 10.
Before -ing -기 전에

Section I - Vocabulary and Comprehension

Change each of the following verbs to nouns, add 전에, and write an English translation.

Example: 사다 ➤ 사기 전에 = *before buying*

1. 오다 ➤   =

2. 마시다 ➤   =

3. 연습하다 ➤   =

4. 주다 ➤   =

5. 씻다 ➤   =

6. 쓰다 ➤   =

7. 보내다 ➤   =

8. 들어오다 ➤   =

9. 열다 ➤   =

10. 팔다 ➤   =

Add 전에 to each of the following nouns and write an English translation.

11. 여섯 시 ➤   =

12. 수업 ➤   =

13. 일요일 ➤   =

14. 여름 휴가 ➤   =

15. 시험 ➤   =

Section II - Reading comprehension

Read the following dialogue and answer the questions.

수영: 우리 내일 몇 시에 만날까요?

태연: 3시쯤에 볼까요?

서현: 3시 전에 만나요. 저 4시에 어디 가야 돼요.

수영: 1시 전에 만나서 점심 먹을까요?

서현: 좋아요.

태연: 저도 좋아요. 저는 아침에 학교 가서 12시 전에 끝나요.

수영: 좋아요. 내일 12시 반까지 다 여기로 오세요.

서현: 내일 유리 씨도 와요?

수영: 유리 씨는 바빠서 못 올 것 같아요. 제가 오늘 자기 전에 유리 씨한테 전화해서 다시 물어볼게요.

16. When did 태연 originally suggest to meet tomorrow?

    a. before 3 o'clock

    b. at 3 o'clock

    c. by 3 o'clock

    d. around 3 o'clock

17. Where does 서현 have to go at 4 o'clock tomorrow?

    a. church

    b. meeting

    c. somewhere (she didn't say exactly where)

    d. school

18. Why did 태연 agree to meet before 1 o'clock tomorrow?

    a. Because she will be busy by 12 o'clock tomorrow.

    b. Because she will not go to school tomorrow.

    c. Because her school will finish before 12 o'clock tomorrow.

    d. none of the above

19. When did 수영 say that she would call 유리?

   a. Before 4 o'clock

   b. Before she goes to bed tonight

   c. She didn't say that she would call 유리.

   d. Before 12:30 tomorrow

Section III - Dictation
Listen to the corresponding MP3 file. Repeat what you hear out loud, then write it down. Each word/phrase will be said twice.

20. Track 23:

21. Track 24:

Lesson 11. ㅂ irregular

ㅂ 불규칙

Section I - Vocabulary

Translate each word to English, then write it in your preferred language (if not English).

1. 돕다 =

2. 어렵다 =

3. 아름답다 =

4. 귀엽다 =

5. 맵다 =

6. 쉽다 =

7. 덥다 =

8. 굽다 =

9. 눕다 =

10. 밉다 =

Section II - Fill in the chart

Using the verbs from the Section I, fill in the chart. The first one has been done for you as an example.

Verb (infinitive)	Present tense	Past tense	Future tense
1a. 돕다	도와요	도왔어요	도울 거예요
2a.			
3a.			
4a.			
5a.			
6a.			
7a.			
8a.			
9a.			
10a.			

Section III - Comprehension

Change the verbs or adjectives into the noun form by adding -(으)ㄴ/는 것 and write an English translation.

11. 돕다 ⟶ _____ = _____

12. 어렵다 ⟶ _____ = _____

13. 아름답다 ⟶ _____ = _____

14. 귀엽다 ⟶ _____ = _____

15. 맵다 ⟶ _____ = _____

16. 쉽다 ⟶ _____ = _____

17. 덥다 ⟶ _____ = _____

18. 굽다 ⟶ _____ = _____

19. 눕다 ⟶ _____ = _____

20. 믿다 ⟶ _____ = _____

Section IV - Conjugation Chart

Conjugate the verbs with the following verb endings, all of which have been covered in previous lessons.

	+ -(으)면	+ -고	+ -아/어/여서
21. 돕다			
22. 입다			
23. 굽다			
24. 잡다			
25. 눕다			
26. 씹다			

Section V - Dictation

Listen to the corresponding MP3 file. Repeat what you hear out loud, then write it down. Each word/phrase will be said twice.

27. Track 25:

28. Track 26:

29. Track 27:

Lesson 12.
But still, nevertheless
그래도

Section I - Vocabulary

Circle the best answer.

1. The Korean word for "to be difficult" is:

    a. 노래방

    b. 쉽다

    c. 어렵다

    d. 공부하다

2. "요즘" means:

    a. these days

    b. dog

    c. cat

    d. yesterday

3. How do you say "money" in Korean?

    a. 머니

    b. 캐시

    c. 저녁

    d. 돈

4. The literal translation for this Korean word is "singing room":

  a. 노래방

  b. 플스방

  c. 게임방

  d. PC방

5. How do you say "soccer" in Korean?

  a. 수영

  b. 농구

  c. 축구

  d. 야구

6. "노래하다" means:

  a. to worry

  b. to be late

  c. to open

  d. to sing

7. "그래" comes from the Korean word:

  a. 그런데

  b. 그렇게 해

  c. 그렇지만

  d. none of these

. The Korean word for "to worry" in the infinitive form is:

   a. 노래하다

   b. 이상하다

   c. 가다

   d. 걱정하다

. "-도" means:

   a. also

   b. too

   c. even

   d. all of the above

. To say "but still", "however", or "nonetheless" in Korean, you use the word:

   a. 근데

   b. 그래도

   c. 그래서

   d. 그렇지만

Section II - Writing practice

Write a second sentence starting with 그래도. Example answers have been provided in the Answer Key.

   Example: 비가 와요. <u>그래도 갈 거예요?</u>

11. 너무 더워요. ~~~~~~~~~~~~~~~~~~~~~~~~~~~~

12. 너무 배불러요. ~~~~~~~~~~~~~~~~~~~~~~~~~~~

13. 요즘 정말 바빠요. ~~~~~~~~~~~~~~~~~~~~~~~~~

14. 집에서 회사까지 진짜 멀어요. ~~~~~~~~~~~~~~~~

15. 윤아 씨가 화장을 전혀 안 했어요. ~~~~~~~~~~~~~
    * 화장 = makeup

Section III - Dictation
Listen to the corresponding MP3 file. Repeat what you hear out loud, then write it down. Each word/phrase will be said twice.

16. Track 28:

17. Track 29:

Adjective in infinitive form	Meaning	+ -(으)ㄴ	Meaning of adjective form
1. 예쁘다	to be pretty	예쁜	pretty
2. 크다			
3. 작다			
4. 행복하다			
5. 슬프다			
6. 피곤하다			
7. 졸리다			
8. 좋다			
9. 귀엽다			
10. 덥다			

Translate the following phrases/sentences to Korean.

11. Pretty woman

   =

12. Big bag

   =

13. Good idea

   =

14. Bad person

   =

15. Cute dog

   =

16. Hot weather

   =

17. Happy cat

   =

18. Do you have a smaller bag?

    =

19. I want to eat something delicious.

    =

20. There are many people here.

    =

Section III - Dictation

Listen to the corresponding MP3 file. Repeat what you hear out loud, then write it down. Each word/phrase will be said twice.

21. Track 30:

22. Track 31:

23. Track 32:

Section I - Comprehension

True/False - Decide if the statement is true or false. If it is false, correct the underlined term or statement so that the statement is true.

1. The meaning of a verb that has been changed into an adjective <u>depends on the context of the sentence.</u>

    ≫

2. In order to conjugate a verb into an adjective, <u>you add ㄴ to the verb stem, such as in 좋아한.</u>

    ≫

3. When the verb stem of a verb ends with ㄹ, <u>you change the ㄹ to ㄴ to make it into an adjective.</u>

    ≫

4. <u>경화가 좋아하는 가수가 여기 있어요.</u> = The singer who likes Kyung-hwa is here.

    ≫

Section II - Complete the dialogue

Fill in the blanks by translating the given English phrase in parenthesis to Korean and writing it on the line provided.

5.

A: 이 노래 좋아해요?

B: 네. _____ 예요.
         (a song that I like)

6.

A: _____ 있어요?
   (a cafe that you go to often)

B: 아니요. 없어요.

7.

A: 저 사람, _____ 이에요?
         (a person that you know)

B: 아니요. _____ 이에요.
         (a person that you don't know)

8.

A: 지금 도서관에서 _____ 많아요?
         (students who are studying)

B: 네. 정말 많아요.

Section III - Dictation

Listen to the corresponding MP3 file. Repeat what you hear out loud, then write it down. Each word/phrase will be said twice.

9. Track 33:

10. Track 34:

Section I - Comprehension

Circle the best answer.

I. 그러면 is a _____, which links words, phrases, and clauses together.

    a. pronoun

    b. conjunction

    c. predicate noun

    d. antecedent

2. Using 그럼 instead of 그러면 is used most often when:

    a. speaking casually

    b. writing

    c. dancing

    d. none of these

3. The word 그러면 is a combination of:

    a. 그런 and -면

    b. 그럼 and -면

    c. 그렇다 and -면

    d. 그래도 and -면

4. 그럼 means:

    a. the same thing as 그러면

    b. the name of a character on the children's TV show "뽀로로"

    c. "in that case", "well then", or "if so"

    d. both A and C

Section II - Complete the dialogue

Read the following conversations. Fill in the blanks using 그러면 and the prompts in parentheses. Be sure to use the correct sentence endings/conjugations. After you have completed the dialogue, translate the entire conversation to English and your preferred language (if not English).

5. A: 오늘 시간 있어요? =

    B: 미안해요. 오늘은 바빠요. =

    A: _____? =
    (시간, 있다, 언제)

6. A: 저 늦었어요! =

    B: _____. =
    * imperative (타다, 택시)

7. A: 너무 더워요. =

    B: _____. =
    * imperative (창문, 열다)

8. A: 같이 나가서 밥 먹을까요? =

    B: 아, 저는 밥 먹고 왔어요. =

    A: ＿＿＿＿＿＿＿＿＿＿＿＿＿. =

    (먹고 오다, 혼자)

9. A: 저 이 가방 살까요? =

    B: 가방이 너무 큰 것 같아요. =

    A: ＿＿＿＿＿＿＿＿＿＿? =

    (이거, 사다)

Section III - Dictation

Listen to the corresponding MP3 file. Repeat what you hear out loud, then write it down. Each word/phrase will be said twice.

10. Track 35:

11. Track 36:

12. Track 37:

Lesson 16.
Let's   -아/어/여요 (청유형)

Section I - Vocabulary

Match each sentence ending to the type of language
in which it is most commonly used.

1. -아/어/여요   a. polite/casual

2. -(으)시죠   b. honorific

3. -자   c. polite/plain

4. -(으)ㄹ래요?   d. informal

5. -(으)실래요?   e. polite/formal

Section II - Conjugation Chart

Conjugate the verbs in the infinitive with the sentence endings introduced in
Section I to express "let's" in Korean.

	+ -아/어/여요.	+ -(으)시죠.	+ -자.	+ -(으)ㄹ래요?	+ -(으)실래요?
6. 시작하다					

7. 가다					
8. 공부하다					
9. 달리다					
10. 눕다					
11. 보다					

Section III - Comprehension

Identify the underlined part of the dialogue as being a form of "let's" or the "plain present tense". Write L for "let's" and P for "plain present tense".

12.

A: 우리 점심 먹어요.

B: 뭐 먹을까요?   ~~~~~~~~~~

13.

A: 둘이 뭐 해요?

B: 같이 공부해요.   ~~~~~~~~~~

14.

A: 내일 몇 시에 만날까요?

B: 세 시에 만나요. ~~~~~~~~~

15.

A: 오늘도 일해요?

B: 네. 오늘도 일해요. ~~~~~~~~~

16.

A: 편의점에 갔다 올게요.

B: 같이 가요! ~~~~~~~~~

Section IV - Dictation

Listen to the corresponding MP3 file. Repeat what you hear out loud, then write it down. Each word/phrase will be said twice.

17. Track 38:

18. Track 39:

Lesson 17.
In order to, for the sake of
위해, 위해서

Section I - Vocabulary

Translate each word to English, then write it in your preferred language (if not English).

1. 회사 =

2. 건강 =

3. 슈퍼맨 =

4. 세계 =

5. 평화 =

6. 열심히 =

7. 부모님 =

8. 모으다 =

9. 운동 =

10. 매일 =

Section II - Writing practice

Write a complete sentence using the two given prompts and -을/를 위해서. Translate each sentence to English and your preferred language (if not English).

Example:

[Present Progressive] 운동을 하다, 건강

➤➤ 건강을 위해서 운동을 하고 있어요.

= I am exercising for my health.

11.   [Past] 선물을 준비하다, 친구

➤➤

12.   [Future] 요리를 하다, 부모님

➤➤

13.   [Present Progressive] 돈을 모으다, 미래

➤➤

Write a complete sentence using the two given prompts and -기 위해서. Translate each sentence to English and your preferred language (if not English).

Example:

[Future] 한국에 가다, 한국어를 공부하다

➤➤ 한국어를 공부하기 위해서 한국에 갈 거예요.

= I will go to Korea in order to study Korean.

14. [Past] 창문을 열다, 청소를 하다

   »

15. [Present Progressive] 열심히 공부하다, 대학에 가다

   »

16. [Future] 지금 자다, 내일 일찍 일어나다

   »

Section III - Dictation
Listen to the corresponding MP3 file. Repeat what you hear out loud, then write it down. Each word/phrase will be said twice.

17. Track 40:

18. Track 41:

19. Track 42:

Lesson 18.
Nothing but, only

밖에 + 부정형

Section I - Vocabulary

Match each Korean word to its English translation.

1. 참치   a. cola

2. 한국인   b. to be, to exist

3. 고양이   c. money

4. 밖   d. Korean [person]

5. 밖에   e. a little bit; some

6. 있다   f. outside

7. 없다   g. cat

8. 못하다   h. to not exist, to not be

9. 조금   i. to be poor at

10. 돈   j. outside something; other than something

11. 콜라   k. tuna

Section II - Translation practice

Translate the following statements to English and your preferred language (if not English).

12. 지금 4,000원밖에 없어요. =

13. 미안해요. 저는 영어밖에 못 해요. =

14. 지금 집에 동생밖에 없어요. =

15. 우리 고양이는 참치밖에 안 먹어요. =

16. 왜 공부밖에 안 해요? =

Section III - Reading Comprehension

Of the two options in parenthesis, underline the most correct or likely answer. If both answers are possible, underline both items.

17. 저는 다 잘 먹어요. 그런데 돼지고기(밖에 / 만) 못 먹어요. * 돼지고기 = pork

18. "TTMIK Level 3 워크북 몇 권 있어요?" "한 권(밖에 / 만) 없어요."

19. 오늘 아침(밖에 / 만) 못 먹어서 너무 배고파요. * 아침 = breakfast

20. 저희는 현금(밖에 / 만) 받아요. 카드는 안 받아요. * 받다 = to accept, to take

21. 지금 집에 저(밖에 / 만) 없어요.

22. 오늘 저녁에 파티 가는 사람 저(밖에 / 만) 없어요?

Section IV - Dictation

Listen to the corresponding MP3 file. Repeat what you hear out loud, then write it down. Each word/phrase will be said twice.

23. Track 43:

24. Track 44:

Lesson 19.
after -ing 다음에, 후에, 뒤에

Section I - Vocabulary and Conjugation

Fill in the chart. The first one has been done for you as an example.

Phrase in infinitive form	Meaning	+ 다음(or 후/뒤)에	Meaning of V+ 다음(or 후/뒤)에
1. 집에 가다	to go home	집에 간 다음에	after going home
2. 커피를 마시다			
3. 학교에 가다			
4. 운동하다			
5. 지하철을 타다			
6. 점심을 먹다			
7. 피아노를 치다			
8. 책을 읽다			

9. 한국어를 공부하다			
10. 편지를 쓰다			

Section II – Translation practice

Translate each sentence to Korean using 다음(or 후/뒤)에.

11. After doing exercise, I ate cake.

   ≫

12. After having lunch, where are we going?

   ≫

13. Let's go to "noraebang" after doing this.

   ≫

14. Shall we go home after drinking coffee?

   ≫

15. Please close the window (for me) after you clean up.

   »

Section III - Comprehension
Rewrite each sentence to include 다음(or 후/뒤)에.

16. 주문하기 전에 얼마인지 보세요.

   »

17. 학교 가기 전에 아침 일찍 만나요.

   »

18. 게임 하기 전에 숙제 먼저 해야 돼요. * 먼저 = first

   »

19. 책 읽기 전에 영화로 먼저 볼 거예요.

   »

20. 친구가 사기 전에 제가 먼저 샀어요.

   »

Section IV - Dictation

Listen to the corresponding MP3 file. Repeat what you hear out loud, then write it down. Each word/phrase will be said twice.

21. Track 45:

22. Track 46:

23. Track 47:

Section I - Vocabulary and Conjugation

Fill in the chart. The first one has been done for you as an example.

Verb or Adjective (infinitive form)	Meaning	+ -아/어/여도	Meaning of V/Adj + -아/어/여도
ex. 하다	to do	해도	even if you do; even though you do
1. 울다			
2. 좋다			
3. 보다			
4. 예쁘다			
5. 바쁘다			
6. 공부하다			
7. 쉽다			
8. 달리다			

9. 비싸다			
10. 좋아하다			

Section II - Comprehension

Complete the sentences using -아/어/여도 together with one of the phrases from the box:

배가 안 고프다   지금 가다   전화하다

조금 비싸다   불을 켜다

11. ＿＿＿＿＿＿＿＿＿＿＿ 사무실이 어두워요.

12. ＿＿＿＿＿＿＿＿＿＿＿ 안 받아요.

13. ＿＿＿＿＿＿＿＿＿＿＿ 이미 늦었어요.

14. ＿＿＿＿＿＿＿＿＿＿＿ 먹어야 돼요.

15. 이 차가 ＿＿＿＿＿＿＿＿＿＿＿ 튼튼해요.

Section III - Writing practice
Combine the two given sentences using -아/어/여도.

16. 이 사과는 예쁘지 않아요. 그래도 맛은 있어요.

>>

17. 책이 커요. 그래도 이 가방에 넣을 수 있어요.

>>

18. 바빠요. 그래도 건강을 위해서 운동은 해야 돼요.

>>

19. 제 친구는 영어는 못해요. 그래도 중국어는 잘해요.

>>

20. 책이 없어요. 그래도 핸드폰으로 공부할 수 있어요.

>>

Talk To Me In Korean Workbook

Section IV - Dictation

Listen to the corresponding MP3 file. Repeat what you hear out loud, then write it down. Each word/phrase will be said twice.

21. Track 48:

22. Track 49:

Section I - Vocabulary

Based on the given English translation, circle the correct spelling of the Korean word.

Example: To worry

거그장하다   컥창하다   걱정하다

1.   To take a shower

셔우와하다   샤워하다   샤월하다

2.   To be big

쿠다   그다   크다

3.   To open

열다   여울다   율다

4.   To be happy

행보가다   행복하다   헹복하다

5. To be sleepy

    졸리다   줄리다   절리다

6. To dance

    줌주다   춤츠다   춤추다

7. To speak; to say; to talk

    말라다   말하다   마라다

8. To be hungry

    베고프다   패고브다   배고프다

9. To practice

    연습하다   연스바다   야느습하다

10. To read

    읽타   읽다   일그다

Section II - Comprehension
Answer the following questions in English.

11. Explain the type of verb each of these linking verbs is attached to and how to conjugate.

-는데:

-은데:

-ㄴ데:

12. List the 6 main types of usages for this set of linking verbs.

Usage 1:

Usage 2:

Usage 3:

Usage 4:

Usage 5:

Usage 6:

Section III - Conjugation
Underline the correct conjugation.

13. 내일 (일요일인데 / 일요일은데 / 일요일는데), 뭐 할 거예요?

14. 어제 자고 (있었인데 / 있었은데 / 있었는데), 한국에서 전화가 왔어요.

15. 아직 (9시인데 / 9시은데 / 9시는데) 벌써 졸려요.

16. 준비 많이 (했인데요 / 했은데요 / 했는데요).

17. (멋있인데요 / 멋있은데요 / 멋있는데요)!

18. 지금 어디에 (있인데요 / 있은데요 / 있는데요)?

19. 지금요? 지금 (바쁜데요 / 바쁘은데요 / 바쁘는데요).

Section IV - Dictation

Listen to the corresponding MP3 file. Repeat what you hear out loud, then write it down. Each word/phrase will be said twice.

20. Track 50:

21. Track 51:

22. Track 52:

Lesson 22.
maybe I might...
-(으)ㄹ 수도 있어요

Section I - Comprehension

True/False - Decide if the statement is true or false. If it is false, correct the underlined term or statement so that the statement is true.

1. The word 수 means "can" or "able".

    »

2. -도 means "too" or "also".

    »

3. -(으)ㄹ 수도 있다 can take on various meanings depending on the context of the sentence, but some of the most common English translations are, "there is a way to do...", "there is an idea for doing...", or "there is a possibility for doing...".

    »

4. Although -(으)ㄹ 수도 있다 could mean "to also be able to do something", it usually means "it might", "it could" or "perhaps".

    »

Section II - Writing

Conjugate the given word with -(으)ㄹ 수도 있다 to create a correct Korean translation for the given statement.

5. might know (something/someone)

=

* to know (something/someone) = 알다

My friend might know (the person/the thing).

=

* to meet = 만나다

6. might meet

=

We might meet again next week.

=

7. might be small

=

* to be small = 작다

The hat might be small.

=

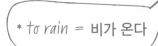
* to rain = 비가 온다

8. might rain

    =

    It might rain this evening.

    =

9. might use

    =

    I might use it later.

    =

* to use = 쓰다

Section III - Dictation

Listen to the corresponding MP3 file. Repeat what you hear out loud, then write it down. Each word/phrase will be said twice.

10. Track 53:

11. Track 54:

12. Track 55:

Lesson 23.
Word Builder #1

학(學)

Section I - Vocabulary, Part 1

Please define/translate each word to English using what you know or a dictionary. Then write it in your preferred language (if not English).

1. 대학교수(大學教授): _____

2. 초등학교(初等學校): _____

3. 생명과학(生命科學): _____

4. 수학(數學): _____

5. 학자(學者): _____

6. 장학금(獎學金): _____

7. 경제학(經濟學): _____

8. 수학여행(修學旅行): _____

9. 지구과학(地球科學): _____

10. 학교(學校): _____

11. 전학(轉學): _____

12. 유학생(留學生): _____

13. 대학교(大學校): _____

14. 어학(語學): _____

15. 학생(學生): _____

16. 복학생(復學生): _____

17. 물리학(物理學): _____

18. 학원(學院): _____

19. 방학(放學): _____

20. 대학원생(大學院生): _____

21. 학교생활(學校生活): _____

22. 고등학교(高等學校): _____

23. 학용품(學用品): _____

24. 중학교(中學校): _____

Section II - Vocabulary, Part 2

Pyramids - Based on 학, build a pyramid with words from Section I.

* Each level reflects the number of syllables in each word to be written.

* Two words go on each level of the pyramid.

* One answer for each level in number 25 have been done for you as an example. Please finish number 25 before you write down the answer for numbers 26~28.

25. People

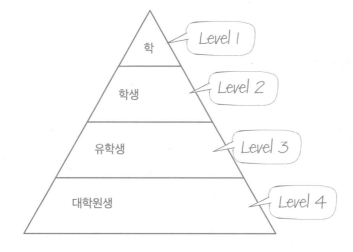

26. Places

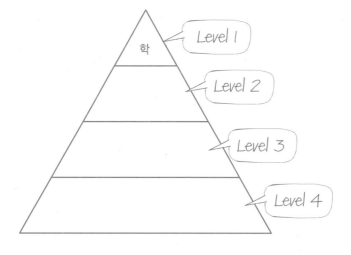

27. Subjects of study

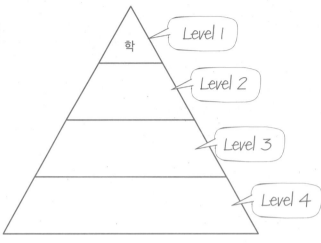

28. Related words

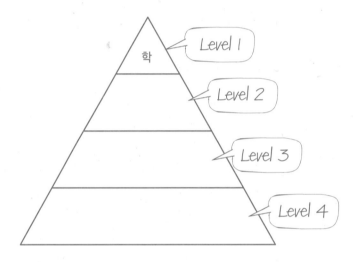

Section III - Dictation

Listen to the corresponding MP3 file. Repeat what you hear out loud, then write it down. Each word/phrase will be said twice.

29. Track 56:

30. Track 57:

Lesson 24.
르 irregular   르 불규칙

Section I - Vocabulary and Comprehension

Fill in the chart as the example demonstrates.

Verb or Adjective	English definition	V/A + -아/어/여요	V/A + -아/어/여서	V/A + -았/었/였어요
ex. 다르다	to be different	달라요	달라서	달랐어요
1. 기르다				
2. 고르다				
3. 누르다				
4. 마르다				
5. 모르다				
6. 바르다				

7. 부르다				
8. 빠르다				
9. 서두르다				
10. 찌르다				

Section II - Comprehension

Translate the following sentences to Korean using one of the words in Section I and the prompts in parenthesis.

11. Push the bell and wait. (벨, -고)

   =

12. It was too fast so I couldn't see it. (못, -아/어/여서)

   =

13. Even though I call (him), there is no answer. (대답, -아/어/여도)

   =

14. I went out of my house before my hair was dry. (나오다, -기 전에)

    =

15. I don't know (about it) well, but why? (잘, -(으)ㄴ/는데)

    =

16. I asked many people in order to choose a good car. (많은, -기 위해서)

    =

Section III - Dictation
Listen to the corresponding MP3 file. Repeat what you hear out loud, then write it down. Each word/phrase will be said twice.

17. Track 58:

18. Track 59:

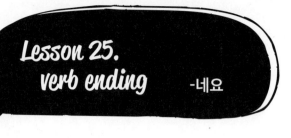

Lesson 25.
verb ending -네요

Section I - Vocabulary

Please define/translate each word to English. Then write it in your preferred language. (if not English)

1. 말: _____

2. 맞다: _____

3. 무겁다: _____

4. 물: _____

5. 깊다: _____

6. 방: _____

7. 항상: _____

8. 더럽다: _____

9. 밤: _____

10. 밝다: _____

Section II - Comprehension

Answer the following questions in English.

11. If you change a plain sentence to the -네요 form, what are you implying/ indicating?

12. How do you conjugate -네요?

13. Can a plain sentence mean the same thing as a sentence ending in -네요?

Section III - Writing practice

Change the plain sentence to the -네요 form.

14. 시험이 너무 어려워요.

    ≫

15. 친구 말이 정말 맞아요.

    ≫

16. 가방이 진짜 무거워요.

   >>

17. 물이 생각보다 깊어요.

   >>

18. 제 방은 항상 더러워요.

   >>

19. 지금 밤 10시인데 아직도 밝아요.

   >>

Section IV - Dictation
Listen to the corresponding MP3 file. Repeat what you hear out loud, then write it down. Each word/phrase will be said twice.

20. Track 60:

21. Track 61:

Lesson 26. ㄷ irregular   ㄷ 불규칙

Section I - Vocabulary

Please translate/define each word to English. Then write it in your preferred language (if not English).

1. 듣다: _____

2. 받다: _____

3. 묻다: _____

4. 닫다: _____

5. 깨닫다: _____

6. 붇다: _____

7. 걷다: _____

8. 싣다: _____

9. 믿다: _____

Section II - Comprehension
Answer the following questions in English.

10. How does ㄷ irregular work?

11. "묻다" has two meanings. Which meaning conjugates in an irregular way?

12. Except for 묻다, there were 3 words introduced in Section I which conjugate in a regular way. What are they?

Section III - Conjugation Chart
Conjugate the following verbs into each tense.

	Present	Past	Future	Present Progressive
13. 듣다				
14. 받다				

15. 묻다				
16. 닫다				
17. 깨닫다				
18. 붇다				
19. 걷다				
20. 싣다				
21. 믿다				

Section IV - Dictation

Listen to the corresponding MP3 file. Repeat what you hear out loud, then write it down. Each word/phrase will be said twice.

22. Track 62:

23. Track 63:

Lesson 27. Politeness Levels

반말 and 존댓말

Section I - Comprehension

1. The ending most associated with 반말 is:

   a. -ㅂ니다

   b. -ㅂ니까

   c. -아/어/여

   d. -(아/어/여)요

2. In which of the following situations should you NOT use 반말?

   a. You don't know the other person. You just met him/her.

   b. You are talking to a large group of people or filming a video blog.

   c. You know the other person only through work, and not personally.

   d. all of the above

3. Up until now, all the sentence endings introduced in the TTMIK lessons have been in the _____ politeness level.

   a. 존댓말

   b. 반말

   c. casual language

   d. crude language

4. You can use 반말 when you are talking to:

    a. your classmates in high school

    b. yourself

    c. your boss

    d. both A and B

5. When addressing someone in _____, it is polite to add the word "씨" after his/her name.

    a. 반말

    b. 잔말

    c. 존댓말

    d. 빈말

Section II – Situational Expressions

Write the appropriate word or phrase to use in each situation.

6. You have just met someone for the first time and you have discovered that he/she is the same age as you. How can you politely ask if you can speak in 반말 with each other?

7. You go to your friend's house for a visit, and his/her parents are there. How do you greet your friend's parents when you see them?

8. Your younger brother, whose given name is 승훈, is playing video games and you want him to help you clean up the house. In order to get his attention, you call out his name. How do you address him?

9. You are in class at Seoul University listening to your professor give a lecture on Beethoven. You have a question that you would like to ask. Would you use 존댓말 or 반말? How would you address the professor?

Section III - Conjugation practice

Conjugate the following sentences into 반말.

10. 이거 뭐예요?

   >>

11. 어제 친구 만났어요.

   >>

12. 우리 내일 쇼핑 갈까요?

   >>

13. 너무 걱정하지 마세요.

    》

14. 저 강남에서 친구 만날 거예요.

    》

Section IV - Dictation
Listen to the corresponding MP3 file. Repeat what you hear out loud, then write it down. Each word/phrase will be said twice.

15. Track 64:

16. Track 65:

17. Track 66:

Section I - Vocabulary

Please define/translate each word to English. Then write it in your preferred language (if not English).

1. 공부하다: _____

2. 기다리다: _____

3. 놀다: _____

4. (transportation) 타다: _____

5. 물어보다: _____

6. 쉬다: _____

7. 청소하다: _____

8. 가다: _____

9. 먹다: _____

10. 산책하다: _____

Section II - Fill in the blank

Complete each conversation by filling in the blank with the most appropriate word from Section I + -자.

11.

A: 벌써 한 시네! 점심 _____.

B: 뭐 먹을까?

A: 성민이한테 _____. 성민아, 뭐 먹고 싶어?

12.

A: 우와! 오늘 날씨 진짜 좋네! 우리 나가서 _____.

B: 나는 피곤한데. 우리 그냥 집에서 _____.

13.

A: 집이 너무 더러운 것 같아. 우리 _____. 창문 좀 열어 줘.

B: 희철이랑 같이 하자. 곧 올 거야. 조금만 _____.

Section III - Comprehension

Change the positive sentences to negative sentences. Then translate each sentence to English and your preferred language (if not English).

14. 이거 사자.

>>

15. 지금 들어가자. * 들어가다 = *to go inside*

   »

16. 점심시간에 영화 보자.

   »

17. 오늘은 일찍 문 닫자.

   »

18. 카페에서 공부하자.

   »

19. 우리 서두르자.

   »

Section IV - Dictation

Listen to the corresponding MP3 file. Repeat what you hear out loud, then fill in the blanks with the missing word. Each phrase will be said twice.

20. Track 67: 우리 역까지 ～～～～～～～～～～～～～～～～～～～～～ .

21. Track 68: 잠깐만! ～～～～～～～～～～～～～～～～～～～ .

22. Track 69: ～～～～～～～～～～～～～～～～～～～～～～ 만나자.

Lesson 29.
ㅅ irregular
ㅅ 불규칙

Section I - Vocabulary

Match each Korean word (in its infinitive form) to its common English translation.

1. 웃다   a. to pour

2. 씻다   b. to smile; to laugh

3. 벗다   c. to draw (a line)

4. 짓다   d. to make, to build, to compose

5. 긋다   e. to wash

6. 잇다   f. to take (clothes) off

7. 낫다   g. to connect, to link

8. 붓다   h. to stir (liquid)

9. 젓다   i. to heal, to recover; to be better

                      (in comparison)

Section II - Conjugation Chart

Conjugate the following verbs into each tense.

	Present	Past	Future	Present Progressive
10. 웃다				
11. 씻다				
12. 벗다				
13. 짓다				
14. 긋다				
15. 잇다				
16. 낫다				
17. 붓다				
18. 젓다				

Section III - Comprehension

Read the following passage about how to make steamed rice. If the underlined phrases or words are conjugated incorrectly, correct them.

* 밥 = steamed rice
* 손 = hand
* 밥솥 = rice cooker
* 취사 버튼 = "cook" button

* 쌀 = rice
* 깨끗하다 = to be clean
* 넣다 = to put in

19. 밥 짓는 것은 전혀 어렵지 않아요. 오늘 아침에 저도 밥을 지었어요. 먼저 쌀을 씻어야 돼요. 쌀을 씻기 위해서 물을 부으세요. 물을 부은 다음에 손으로 젓으세요. 쌀을 다 씻었으면 그 물만 버리세요. 쌀에 다시 깨끗한 물을 부어서 밥솥에 넣으세요. 그리고 취사 버튼을 누르세요. 그러면 끝나요. 쉽지 않아요?

   ≫

Section IV - Dictation

Listen to the corresponding MP3 file. Repeat what you hear out loud, then write it down. Each word/phrase will be said twice.

20. Track 70:

21. Track 71:

22. Track 72:

Section I - Vocabulary, Part 1

Please define/translate each word to English using what you know or a dictionary. Then write it in your preferred language (if not English).

1. 화장실(化粧室): _____

2. 실외(室外): _____

3. 실내(室內): _____

4. 실장(室長): _____

5. 교무실(教務室): _____

6. 사무실(事務室): _____

7. 미용실(美容室): _____

8. 병실(病室): _____

9. 회의실(會議室): _____

10. 대기실(待機室): _____

11. 연습실(練習室):

_____

12. 교실(敎室):

_____

13. 침실(寢室):

_____

14. 거실(居室):

_____

15. 응급실(應急室):

_____

16. 조리실(調理室):

_____

17. 수술실(手術室):

_____

18. 강의실(講義室):

_____

19. 휴게실(休憩室):

_____

20. 양호실(養護室):

_____

21. 교장실(校長室):

_____

22. 오락실(娛樂室):

_____

23. 흡연실(吸煙室):

_____

Section II - Vocabulary, Part 2

Complete the vocabulary web by filling in the blanks with words from the Word Bank most commonly associated with each of the categories. All words were defined in Section I.

Word Bank

교실	거실	강의실	침실
수술실	병실	양호실	응급실
사무실	교장실	회의실	교무실

24.

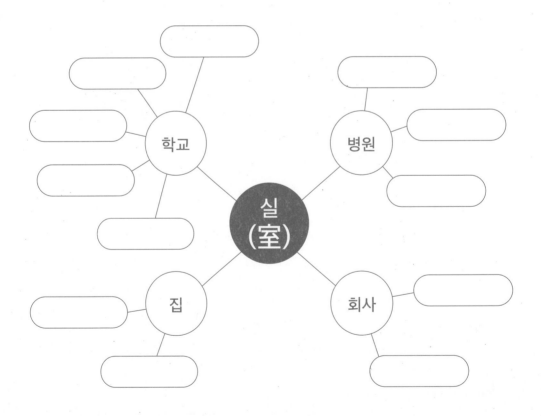

Section III - Dictation

Listen to the corresponding MP3 file. Repeat what you hear out loud, then fill in the blanks with the missing word. Each phrase will be said twice.

25. Track 73: 지금 _____ 누구 있어요?

26. Track 74: _____ 거울이 _____.

27. Track 75: _____ 냄새가 나요.

Answer Key
for
TTMIK
Workbook
Level 3

Lesson 1

Section I – Vocabulary

1. to be expensive

2. to be big

3. to be noisy

4. to be hot

5. to be fast

6. to be difficult

7. to be sad

8. to be easy

9. to be bitter

10. to be salty

11. to be spicy

12. to be tasty; to be delicious

Section II - Writing practice

1a. 너무 비싸요.

= It's too expensive.

2a. 너무 커요.

= It's too big.

3a. 너무 시끄러워요.

= It's too noisy.

4a. 너무 더워요.

= It's too hot.

5a. 너무 빨라요.

= It's too fast.

6a. 너무 어려워요.

= It's too difficult.

7a. 너무 슬퍼요.

= It's too sad.

8a. 너무 쉬워요.

= It's too easy.

9a. 너무 써요.

= It's too bitter.

10a. 너무 짜요.

= It's too salty.

11a. 너무 매워요.

= It's too spicy.

12a. 너무 맛있어요.

= It's really delicious.

Section III - Dictation

13. 음악 소리가 너무 커요.

= The music is too loud.

14. 신발이 너무 작아요.

= The shoes are too small.

Lesson 2

Section I - Vocabulary

1. b

2. d

3. f

4. h

5. j

6. i

7. g

8. e

9. a

10. c

Section II - Comprehension

11.

-고 is attached to the end of a verb stem and

links verbs, phrases, and sentences. It has

the same meaning as 그리고, which means "and" or "and then".

12.

When you make a compound sentence in English using the conjunction "and" to connect smaller sentences, you need to make the tenses of the verbs agree. However, in Korean, that's not absolutely necessary, and sometimes it sounds unnatural to try to use the same tenses for every verb, especially the future tense and the past tense. Most native Korean speakers just use the past tense or the future tense in only the final verb.

13.

Because -고 has the meaning of "and after that" or "and then".

Section III - Writing practice

14. 10월에는 일본에 가고, 11월에는 미국에 갈 거예요.

15. 오늘은 커피숍에서 친구를 만나고, 한국어 공부했어요.

16. 삼겹살 먹고, 김치 먹고, 마늘 먹고, 고추 먹고, 밥 먹었어요. 지금 배가 너무 불러요.

17. 수영하고, 영어 공부하고, 점심 먹었어요.

Section IV - Dictation

18. 이 책은 재미있고 싸요.

= This book is interesting and cheap.

19. 집에 가서 씻고 잤어요.

= After I got home, I took a shower and slept.

Lesson 3

Section I - Vocabulary

1. d

2. a

3. b

4. e

5. c

Section II - Complete the dialogue

6. 앞에

7. 위에, 밑에

8. 밑에, 밑에, 뒤에

Section III - Listening skills

9. 은행은 학교 뒤에 있어요.

= The bank is behind the school.

10. 강아지는 자동차 옆에 있어요.

= The dog is next to the car.

11. 컴퓨터는 책상 위에 있어요.

= The computer is on top of the desk.

Lesson 4

Section I - Comprehension

1. True

2. True

3. False - 올까요?

Section II - Vocabulary and Conjugation

4. to drink

마실까요?

5. to start

시작할까요?

6. to put, to place

놓을까요?

7. to run

달릴까요?

8. to make

만들까요?

9. to sit

앉을까요?

Section III - Complete the sentence

10. 책을 어디에 놓을까요?

= Where shall I put the book?

11. 언제 다시 전화할까요?

= When shall I call you again?

12. 산에 갈까요?

= Shall we go to the mountain?

13. 내일 비가 올까요?

= Do you think it will rain tomorrow?

/ I wonder if it will rain tomorrow.

14. 여기에서 사진 찍을까요?

= Shall we take a picture here?

Section IV - Dictation

15. 이 사람은 누구일까요?

= Who do you think this person is?

/ I wonder who this person is.

16. 내일 우리 영화 볼까요?

= Shall we see a movie tomorrow?

/ Do you want to see a movie together

tomorrow?

17. 커피 마실까요? 차 마실까요?

= Shall we drink coffee? Shall we drink tea?

/ Do you want to drink coffee or tea?

Lesson 5

Section I - Vocabulary and Comprehension

1. d

2. c

3. c

4. b

5. d

6. c

7. a

8. c

9. d

10. d

11. a

Section II - Complete the dialogue

12. 100명쯤 있어요.

13. 20,000원쯤 있어요.

14. 몇 시쯤 갈 거예요?

15. 내일 몇 시쯤 만날까요?

Section III - Dictation

16. 독일에서 2년 정도 살았어요.

= I lived in Germany for about 2 years.

17. 집이 어디쯤이에요?

= Whereabouts is your house?

Lesson 6

Section I - Comprehension

1.

With -(으)ㄹ 거예요, you are expressing your intention or plan for a future action or your expectation for a future state which is not related to or affected by the reaction or request of the person you're talking to. However, -(으)ㄹ 게요 expresses the future but pertains to your actions or decisions as a reaction to or as a result of what the other person says or thinks.

2.

a. When you are changing your plan according to what the other person said.

b. When you want to check what the other person thinks by saying something and seeing their reaction.

c. When you decide to do something because of something the other person said.

Section II - Translation Practice

3. 공원에 갈 거예요.

4. 저도 갈게요.

5. 내일 전화할게요.

6. 경화 씨는 나갈 거예요.

7. 지금 나갈게요.

Section III - Reading Comprehension

8. 할 거예요, 갈 거예요

9. 줄게요

10. 공부할 거예요, 도와줄게요

Section IV - Dictation

11. 청소는 제가 할게요. = I will do the cleaning. / As for the cleaning, I will do it.

12. 지금 주문할게요. = I will order now.

13. 제가 다 먹을게요. = I will eat them all.

Lesson 7

Section I - Comprehension

1. 아파서 / Jimin was sick, so she went home.

2. 모아서 / What are you going to do with the money you save up?

3. 가서 / I want to go home as soon as possible and get some rest.

4. 먹어서 / I ate too much, so I am full.

5. 공부해서 / I am going to study hard and I will get a scholarship.

6. 와서 / Come here and look at this.

Section II - Writing practice

7. 오늘은 바빠서 영화를 못 봐요.

8. 공원에 가서 책을 읽을 거예요.

9. 친구를 만나서 밥을 먹었어요.

10. 케이크를 사서 친구한테 줄 거예요.

Section III - Translation practice

11. 한국에 가서 뭐 할 거예요?

12. 서울에 와서 좋아요/기뻐요.

13. 비가 와서 집에 있었어요.

14. 요즘에 바빠서 친구들을 못 만나요.

15. 잠을 많이 자서 전혀 피곤하지 않아요.

= I slept a lot so I am not tired at all.

16. 예를 들어서 설명해 주세요.

= Please explain it by giving me an example.

/Please explain it to me with an example.

Lesson 8

Section I - Vocabulary

1. j

2. f

3. g

4. d

5. h

6. i

7. a

8. c

9. e

10. b

Section II - Translation Practice

11. Hyunwoo is like a robot.

12. The viola is similar to the violin.

13. Hyojin seems to be a genius.

14. This bag and that bag over there are the same.

Section III - Reading comprehension

15. 서울

16. (서울 날씨는) 도쿄 날씨하고 비슷해요.

17. 서울

18. 효진 (씨)

19. 밥을 먹었어요.

20. 나이가 같아요.

Section IV - Dictation

21. 이 강아지는 고양이 같아요.

= This puppy is like a cat.

22. 그 이야기는 거짓말 같아요.

= That story sounds like a lie.

Lesson 9

Section I - Vocabulary

1. to tell; to talk

2. to be expensive

3. to be so; to be that way

4. to be far

5. to be pretty

6. eyes; snow

7. to be strange

Section II - Conjugation chart

8. to talk, to speak; to say

말한 것 같아요

말하는 것 같아요

말할 것 같아요

9. to get up; to wake up

일어난 것 같아요

일어나는 것 같아요

일어날 것 같아요

10. to sleep

잔 것 같아요

자는 것 같아요

잘 것 같아요

11. to study

공부한 것 같아요

공부하는 것 같아요

공부할 것 같아요

12. to buy, to purchase

산 것 같아요

사는 것 같아요

살 것 같아요

13. to practice

연습한 것 같아요

연습하는 것 같아요

연습할 것 같아요

14. to do one's homework

숙제를 한 것 같아요

숙제를 하는 것 같아요

숙제를 할 것 같아요

15. to save up money

돈을 모은 것 같아요

돈을 모으는 것 같아요

돈을 모을 것 같아요

16. to snow

눈이 온 것 같아요

눈이 오는 것 같아요

눈이 올 것 같아요

Section III - Comprehension

17. b

18. c

19. d

20. c

21. d

22. a

Section IV - Dictation

23. 혜미 씨는 아직 모르는 것 같아요.

= It seems that Hyemi doesn't know yet.

 / I think Hyemi doesn't know yet.

24. 그 사람은 요즘 바쁜 것 같아요.

= That person seems busy these days.

 / I think that person is busy these days.

25. 그것도 괜찮을 것 같아요.

= It seems that it will also be okay.

 / I think it will also be okay.

Lesson 10

Section I - Vocabulary and Comprehension

1. 오기 전에 = before coming

2. 마시기 전에 = before drinking

3. 연습하기 전에 = before practicing

4. 주기 전에 = before giving

5. 씻기 전에 = before washing

6. 쓰기 전에 = before writing; before using

7. 보내기 전에 = before sending

8. 들어오기 전에 = before coming in

9. 열기 전에 = before opening

10. 팔기 전에 = before selling

11. 여섯 시 전에 = before 6 o'clock

12. 수업 전에 = before class

13. 일요일 전에 = before Sunday

14. 여름 휴가 전에 = before summer vaca-
tion/holiday/break

15. 시험 전에 = before the exam

Section II - Reading comprehension

16. d

17. c

18. c

19. b

Section III - Dictation

20. 들어오기 전에 노크하세요.

= Knock before you come in.

21. 사기 전에 잘 생각하세요.

= Think well before you buy it.

Lesson 11

Section I - Vocabulary

1. to help

2. to be difficult

3. to be beautiful

4. to be cute

5. to be spicy

6. to be easy

7. to be hot (weather)

8. to bake

9. to lie down

10. to hate; to be dislikeable

Section II - Fill in the chart

2a. 어렵다

어려워요

어려웠어요

어려울 거예요

3a. 아름답다

아름다워요

아름다웠어요

아름다울 거예요

4a. 귀엽다

귀여워요

귀여웠어요

귀여울 거예요

5a. 맵다

매워요

매웠어요

매울 거예요

6a. 쉽다

쉬워요

쉬웠어요

쉬울 거예요

7a. 덥다

더워요

더웠어요

더울 거예요

8a. 굽다

구워요

구웠어요

구울 거예요

9a. 눕다

누워요

누웠어요

누울 거예요

10a. 밉다

미워요

미웠어요

미울 거예요

Section III - Comprehension

11. 돕는 것

= helping; the act of helping

12. 어려운 것

= being difficult; something difficult; the
   thing that is difficult

13. 아름다운 것

= being beautiful; something beautiful; the
   thing that is beautiful

14. 귀여운 것

= being cute; something cute; the thing that
   is cute

15. 매운 것

= being spicy; something spicy; the thing
   that is spicy

16. 쉬운 것

= being easy; something easy; the thing that
   is easy

17. 더운 것

= being hot (weather)

18. 굽는 것

= baking; the act of baking; the thing that
   you bake; what you bake

19. 눕는 것

= lying down; the act of lying down

20. 미운 것

= something dislikeable; the thing that you
   hate

Section IV - Conjugation Chart

21. 도우면
    돕고
    도와서

22. 입으면
    입고
    입어서

23. 구우면
    굽고
    구워서

24. 잡으면
    잡고
    잡아서

25. 누우면
    눕고
    누워서

26. 씹으면
    씹고
    씹어서

Section V - Dictation

27. 어제는 정말 추웠어요.

= It was really cold yesterday.

   / As for yesterday, it was really cold.

28. 이거 너무 귀여워요.

= This is so cute.

29. 이번 시험은 어려울 거예요.

= This (upcoming) exam will be difficult.

   / This (upcoming) exam is going to be
   difficult.

Lesson 12

Section I - Vocabulary

1. c

2. a

3. d

4. a

5. c

6. d

7. b

8. d

9. d

10. b

Section II - Writing practice

Example answers:

11. 너무 더워요. 그래도 저는 겨울보다 여름이
    더 좋아요.

12. 너무 배불러요. 그래도 더 먹을 수 있어요.

13. 요즘 정말 바빠요. 그래도 행복해요.

14. 집에서 회사까지 진짜 멀어요. 그래도 힘들
    지 않아요.

15. 윤아 씨가 화장을 전혀 안 했어요. 그래도
    너무 예뻤어요.

Section III - Dictation

16. 한국어는 어려워요. 그래도 재미있어요.

= Korean is difficult. But still, it is interesting.

17. 일이 늦게 끝날 거예요. 그래도 기다려 줄
    수 있어요?

= I will get off work late. Nevertheless, can
  you still wait for me?

Lesson 13

Section I - Vocabulary and Comprehension

2. to be big

   큰

   big

3. to be small

   작은

   small

4. to be happy

   행복한

   happy

5. to be sad

   슬픈

   sad

6. to be tired

   피곤한

   tired

7. to be sleepy

   졸린

   sleepy

8. to be good

   좋은

   good

9. to be cute

   귀여운

   cute

10. to be hot (weather)

    더운

    hot

Section II - Translation practice

11. 예쁜 여자

12. 큰 가방

13. 좋은 아이디어 or 좋은 생각

14. 나쁜 사람

15. 귀여운 개

16. 더운 날씨

17. 행복한 고양이

18. 더 작은 가방 있어요?

19. 맛있는 것/거 먹고 싶어요.

20. 여기 많은 사람들이 있어요. or 여기 사람들
이 많아요.

Section III - Dictation

21. 하얀 피아노가 너무 예뻐요.

= The white piano is really pretty.

22. 단 거 좋아해요?

= Do you like sweets? / Do you like sweet
things?

23. 그런 이야기 많이 들었어요.

= I have heard of such things a lot. / People
have said that a lot.

Lesson 14

Section I - Comprehension

1. True

2. False - you add 는 to the verb stem, such
as in 좋아하는

3. False - you drop the ㄹ and add 는

4. False - 경화를 좋아하는 가수가 여기 있어요.

Section II - Complete the dialogue

5. 제가 좋아하는 노래

6. 자주 가는 카페

7. 아는 사람, 모르는 사람

8. 공부하고 있는 학생들

Section III - Dictation

9. 눈이 오는 날에는 영화 보고 싶어요.

= On a day when it snows, I want to see a
movie.

10. 저 소파 위에서 자고 있는 사람 누구예요?

= Who is the person sleeping on the couch
over there?

Lesson 15

Section I - Comprehension

1. b

2. a

3. c

4. d

Section II - Complete the dialogue

5.

A: 오늘 시간 있어요?

= Do you have time today?

B: 미안해요. 오늘은 바빠요.

= Sorry. I'm busy today.

A: 그러면 언제 시간 있어요?

= Then when do you have time?

6.

A: 저 늦었어요!

= I'm late!

B: 그러면 택시 타세요.

= Then take a taxi.

7.

A: 너무 더워요.

= It's too hot.

B: 그러면 창문(을) 여세요.

= Then open the window.

8.

A: 같이 나가서 밥 먹을까요?

= Shall we go out together and have a meal?

B: 아, 저는 밥 먹고 왔어요.

= Oh, I [already] had a meal and came [here].

A: 그러면 혼자 먹고 올게요.

= Then I will eat alone and come.

9.

A: 저 이 가방 살까요?

= Shall I buy this bag?

B: 가방이 너무 큰 것 같아요.

= I think the bag is too big.

A: 그러면 이거 살까요?

= Then shall I buy this one?

Section III - Dictation

10. 그럼 저는 이제 갈게요.

= Well then, I will get going now. / Well then,
   I will leave now.

11. 그럼 이제 어떻게 해요?

= If so, what do we do now?

12. 그러면 저 주세요.

= If so, please give it to me.

Lesson 16

Section I - Vocabulary

1. c

2. b

3. d

4. a

5. e

Section II - Conjugation Chart

6. 시작해요.

시작하시죠.

시작하자.

시작할래요?

시작하실래요?

7. 가요.

가시죠.

가자.

갈래요?

가실래요?

8. 공부해요.

공부하시죠.

공부하자.

공부할래요?

공부하실래요?

9. 달려요.

달리시죠.

달리자.

달릴래요?

달리실래요?

10. 누워요.

누우시죠.

눕자.

누울래요?

누우실래요?

11. 봐요.

보시죠.

보자.

볼래요?

보실래요?

Section III - Comprehension

12. L

13. P

14. L

15. P

16. L

Section IV - Dictation

17. 우리 내일부터 같이 운동해요.

= Let's exercise together [starting] from
tomorrow.

18. 이거 너무 무거워요. 같이 들어요.

= This is too heavy. Let's carry it together.

Lesson 17

Section I - Vocabulary

1. company

2. health

3. Superman

4. world

5. peace

6. (adverb) hard, diligently

7. parents

8. to gather, to collect; to save up

9. exercise; sports

10. every day

Section II - Writing practice

11. 친구를 위해서 선물을 준비했어요.

= I prepared a present for my friend.

12. 부모님을 위해서 요리를 할 거예요.

= I will cook for my parents.

13. 미래를 위해서 돈을 모으고 있어요.

= I am saving up money for the future.

14. 청소를 하기 위해서 창문을 열었어요.

= I opened the window in order to clean up.

15. 대학에 가기 위해서 열심히 공부하고 있어요.

= I am studying hard in order to go to college.

16. 내일 일찍 일어나기 위해서 지금 잘 거예요.

= I am going to bed now in order to get up early
tomorrow.

Section III - Dictation

17. 빨리 가기 위해서 택시를 탔어요.

= I took a taxi in order to get there fast.

18. 저는 피부를 위해서 물을 많이 마셔요.

= I drink a lot of water for my skin.

19. 가족들한테 보내기 위해서 편지를 썼어요.

= I wrote a letter in order to send to my family.

Lesson 18

Section I - Vocabulary

1. k

2. d

3. g

4. f

5. j

6. b

7. h

8. i

9. e

10. c

11. a

Section II - Translation practice

12. I only have 4,000 won now.

13. Sorry. I only speak English.

14. Only my younger brother/sister is at home now.

15. My cat only eats tuna.

16. Why do you only study?

Section III - Reading Comprehension

17. 만

18. 밖에

19. 밖에

20. 만

21. 밖에, 만

22. 밖에

Section IV - Dictation

23. 현우 씨는 일밖에 모르는 사람이에요.

= Hyunwoo is the person who only thinks/
cares/knows about work.

24. 그거 저밖에 몰라요.

= Only I know that.

Lesson 19

Section I - Vocabulary and Conjugation

2. to drink coffee

커피를 마신 다음(or 후/뒤)에

after drinking coffee

3. to go to school

학교에 간 다음(or 후/뒤)에

after going to school

4. to do exercise

운동을 한 다음(or 후/뒤)에

after doing exercise

5. to take/ride on the subway

지하철을 탄 다음(or 후/뒤)에

after taking/riding on the subway

6. to have lunch

점심을 먹은 다음(or 후/뒤)에

after having lunch

7. to play the piano

피아노를 친 다음(or 후/뒤)에

after playing the piano

8. to read a book

책을 읽은 다음(or 후/뒤)에

after reading a book

9. to study Korean

한국어를 공부한 다음(or 후/뒤)에

after studying Korean

10. to write a letter

편지를 쓴 다음(or 후/뒤)에

after writing a letter

Section II - Translation practice

11. 운동한 다음(or 후/뒤)에 케이크를 먹었어요.

12. 점심 먹은 다음(or 후/뒤)에 우리 어디 갈 거
예요?

13. 이거 한 다음(or 후/뒤)에 노래방 가요.

14. 커피 마신 다음(or 후/뒤)에 집에 갈까요?

15. 청소한 다음(or 후/뒤)에 창문 닫아 주세요.

Section III - Comprehension

16. 얼마인지 본 다음(or 후/뒤)에 주문하세요.

17. 아침 일찍 만난 다음(or 후/뒤)에 학교 가요.

18. 숙제 먼저 한 다음(or 후/뒤)에 게임 해야
돼요.

19. 영화로 먼저 본 다음(or 후/뒤)에 책 읽을 거
예요.

20. 제가 먼저 산 다음(or 후/뒤)에 친구가 샀
어요.

Section IV - Dictation

21. 결정한 후에 연락 주세요.

= Contact me after you decide.

22. 그 책 다 읽은 다음에 저 주세요.

= After you finish reading the book, please give it to me.

23. 다 집에 간 뒤에 제가 도착했어요.

= After everyone had [already] gone home, I arrived.

Lesson 20

Section I - Vocabulary and Conjugation

1. to cry

울어도

even if you cry; even though you cry

2. to be good

좋아도

even if it is good; even though it is good

3. to see

봐도

even if you see; even though you see

4. to be pretty

예뻐도

even if you are pretty; even though you are pretty

5. to be busy

바빠도

even if you are busy; even though you are busy

6. to study

공부해도

even if you study; even though you study

7. to be easy

쉬워도

even if it is easy; even though it is easy

8. to run

달려도

even if you run; even though you run

9. to be expensive

비싸도

even if it is expensive; even though it is expensive

10. to like

좋아해도

even if you like it; even though you like it

Section II - Comprehension

11. 불을 켜도 사무실이 어두워요.

12. 전화해도 안 받아요.

13. 지금 가도 이미 늦었어요.

14. 배가 안 고파도 먹어야 돼요.

15. 이 차가 조금 비싸도 튼튼해요.

Section III - Writing practice

16. 이 사과는 예쁘지 않아도 맛은 있어요.

17. 책이 커도 이 가방에 넣을 수 있어요.

18. 바빠도 건강을 위해서 운동은 해야 돼요.

19. 제 친구는 영어는 못해도 중국어는 잘해요.

20. 책이 없어도 핸드폰으로 공부할 수 있어요.

Section IV - Dictation

21. 냄새는 이상해도 맛있어요.

= Even though it smells weird, it's tasty.

22. 침대에 누워도 잠이 안 와요.

= Even though I lie down on my bed, I can't fall

    asleep.

Lesson 21

Section I - Vocabulary

1. 샤워하다

2. 크다

3. 열다

4. 행복하다

5. 졸리다

6. 춤추다

7. 말하다

8. 배고프다

9. 연습하다

10. 읽다

Section II - Comprehension

11.

-는데 is used after verbs, after 있다 and 없다, and after -았 or -겠.

-은데 is used after adjectives that have any final consonant, except ㄹ, in the infinitive form.

-ㄴ데 is used after adjectives that end in a vowel or the consonant ㄹ (in this case, ㄹ is dropped), and after 이다 and 아니다.

12.

Usage 1: Explaining the background or the situation before making a suggestion, a request, or a question.

Usage 2: Explaining the situation before explaining what happened.

Usage 3: Showing a result or situation that is contrasted from the previous action or situation.

Usage 4: Showing surprise or exclamation.

Usage 5: Asking a question. (expecting some explanation about a situation or behavior)

Usage 6: Expecting an answer or a response.

Section III - Conjugation

13. 일요일인데

14. 있었는데

15. 9시인데

16. 했는데요

17. 멋있는데요

18. 있는데요

19. 바쁜데요

Section IV - Dictation

20. 내일 친구 생일인데, 선물을 아직 못 샀어요.

= It's my friend's birthday tomorrow, but I

    haven't been able to buy a present yet.

21. 오늘 뉴스에서 봤는데, 그거 진짜예요?

= I saw it in the news today. Is that for real?

22. 저는 지금 학생인데, 일도 하고 있어요.

= I am a student now, but I'm also working.

Lesson 22

Section I - Comprehension

1. False - "way", "method", or "idea".

2. True

3. False - -(으)ㄹ 수 있다

4. True

Section II - Writing

5. 알 수도 있다, 제 친구가 알 수도 있어요.

6. 만날 수도 있다, 우리 다음 주에 다시 만날 수
   도 있어요.

7. 작을 수도 있다, 모자가 작을 수도 있어요.

8. 비가 올 수도 있다, 오늘 저녁에 비가 올 수
   도 있어요.

9. 쓸 수도 있다, 그거 나중에 쓸 수도 있어요.

Section III - Dictation

10. 이거 가짜일 수도 있어요.

= This might be fake.

11. 정말 그럴 수도 있어요.

= It might really be so.

12. 저 내일 못 올 수도 있어요.

= I might not be able to come here tomorrow.

Lesson 23

Section I - Vocabulary, Part 1

1. university professor

2. elementary school

3. life science

4. mathematics

5. scholar

6. scholarship

7. economics

8. school trip

9. earth science

10. school

11. to change schools

12. student studying abroad

13. university, college

14. language learning

15. student

16. student who has returned to school (usually) after a long break

17. physics

18. private institute

19. school vacation

20. graduate student

21. school life

22. high school; senior high school

23. school supplies; stationery

24. middle school; junior high school

Section II - Vocabulary, Part 2

25. People

26. Places

27. Subjects of study

28. Related words

Section III - Dictation

29. 오늘 학교에 전학생이 왔어요.

= Today a new student came (from another school) to our school.

30. 수학여행은 언제 가요?

= When do you go on a school trip? / When are we going on a school trip?

Lesson 24

Section I - Vocabulary and Comprehension

1. to raise

길러요

길러서

길렀어요

2. to choose

골라요

골라서

골랐어요

3. to press, to push

눌러요

눌러서

눌렀어요

4. to dry (up); to be skinny

말라요

말라서

말랐어요

5. to not know

몰라요

몰라서

몰랐어요

6. to rub, to put on

발라요

발라서

발랐어요

7. to call, to address; to sing

불러요

불러서

불렀어요

8. to be fast

빨라요

빨라서

빨랐어요

9. to hurry

서둘러요

서둘러서

서둘렀어요

10. to stab; to stick

찔러요

찔러서

찔렀어요

Section II - Comprehension

11. 벨을 누르고 기다리세요.

12. 너무 빨라서 못 봤어요.

13. 불러도 대답이 없어요.

14. 머리가 마르기 전에 집을 나왔어요.

15. 저는 잘 모르는데, 왜요?

16. 좋은 차를 고르기 위해서 많은 사람들한테

물어봤어요.

Section III - Dictation

17. 저희 가족은 강아지 두 마리를 기르고 있

어요.

= My family is raising two puppies.

18. 너무 서두르지 마세요.

= Don't rush too much.

Lesson 25

Section I - Vocabulary

1. language; what one says, expression;

word, term

2. to be correct, to be right

3. to be heavy

4. water

5. to be deep

6. room

7. always, all the time

8. to be dirty

9. night

10. to be bright

Section II - Comprehension

11.

You indicate that you are expressing your im-

pression, thought, or surprise.

12.

You add -네요 after the verb stem or the past

tense suffix.

13.

Yes. A plain sentence can mean the same thing

when said with the right intonation, but it

cannot convey the same message when it is

written.

Section III - Writing practice

14. 시험이 너무 어렵네요.

15. 친구 말이 정말 맞네요.

16. 가방이 진짜 무겁네요.

17. 물이 생각보다 깊네요.

18. 제 방은 항상 더럽네요.

19. 지금 밤 10시인데 아직도 밝네요.

Section IV - Dictation

20. 석진 씨, 빨리 왔네요.

= Oh, Seokjin, you got here early.

21. 벌써 11월이네요.

= Wow, it's already November!

Lesson 26

Section I - Vocabulary

1. to hear, to listen

2. to get, to receive, to accept, to take

3. to ask, to bury

4. to close

5. to realize

6. to swell (up), to be bloated

7. to walk

8. to load

9. to believe, to trust

Section II - Comprehension

10.

When the Korean letter ㄷ is the 받침 (the final consonant at the end of a syllable) of a verb stem and is followed by a vowel, ㄷ is changed to ㄹ.

11. 묻다 meaning "to ask"

12. 받다, 닫다, 믿다

Section III - Conjugation Chart

13. 들어요

들었어요

들을 거예요

듣고 있어요

14. 받아요

받았어요

받을 거예요

받고 있어요

15. 물어요(=to ask)/묻어요(=to bury)

물었어요/묻었어요

물을 거예요/묻을 거예요

묻고 있어요/묻고 있어요

16. 닫아요

닫았어요

닫을 거예요

닫고 있어요

17. 깨달아요

깨달았어요

깨달을 거예요

깨닫고 있어요

18. 불어요

불었어요

불을 거예요

붇고 있어요

19. 걸어요

걸었어요

걸을 거예요

걷고 있어요

20. 실어요

실었어요

실을 거예요

싣고 있어요

21. 믿어요

믿었어요

믿을 거예요

믿고 있어요

Section IV - Dictation

22. 걷는 것을 좋아해서 한 시간 동안 걸었어요.

= I like walking, so I walked for one hour.

23. 많이 걸었는데, 안 피곤해요.

= I walked a lot, but I am not tired.

Lesson 27

Section I - Comprehension

1. c

2. d

3. a

4. d

5. c

Section II - Situational Expressions

6. 우리 말 놓을까요? or 말 편하게 해도 되죠?

7. 안녕하세요.

8. 승훈아!

9. 존댓말, 교수님

Section III - Conjugation practice

10. 이거 뭐야?

11. 어제 친구 만났어.

12. 우리 내일 쇼핑 갈까?

13. 너무 걱정하지 마.

14. 나 강남에서 친구 만날 거야.

Section IV - Dictation

15. 그거는 내가 할게.

= As for that, I will do it.

16. 그럼 한국에는 언제 와?

= Well then, when are you coming to Korea?

17. 내일 늦지 마!

= Don't be late tomorrow!

Lesson 28

Section I - Vocabulary

1. to study

2. to wait

3. to hang out, to play

4. to take (a ride); to get on/in

5. to ask

6. to get rest

7. to clean (up)

8. to go

9. to eat

10. to take a walk

Section II - Fill in the blank

11. 먹자, 물어보자

12. 산책하자 or 놀자, 쉬자

13. 청소하자, 기다리자

Section III - Comprehension

14. 이거 사지 말자.

= Let's not buy this.

15. 지금 들어가지 말자.

= Let's not go inside now.

16. 점심시간에 영화 보지 말자.

= Let's not see a movie during lunch break.

17. 오늘은 일찍 문 닫지 말자.

= Today, let's not close the door early.

18. 카페에서 공부하지 말자.

= Let's not study at a cafe.

19. 우리 서두르지 말자.

= Let's not rush.

20. 우리 역까지 걸어가자.

= Let's walk to the subway station.

21. 잠깐만! 같이 나가자.

= Wait! Let's go out together.

22. 우리 내일은 좀 일찍 만나자.

= Let's meet a little early tomorrow.

Lesson 29

Section I - Vocabulary

1. b

2. e

3. f

4. d

5. c

6. g

7. i

8. a

9. h

Section II - Conjugation Chart

10. 웃어요

웃었어요

웃을 거예요

웃고 있어요

11. 씻어요

씻었어요

씻을 거예요

씻고 있어요

12. 벗어요

벗었어요

벗을 거예요

벗고 있어요

13. 지어요

지었어요

지을 거예요

짓고 있어요

14. 그어요

그었어요

그을 거예요

긋고 있어요

15. 이어요

이었어요

이을 거예요

잇고 있어요

16. 나아요

나았어요

나을 거예요

낫고 있어요

17. 부어요

부었어요

부을 거예요

붓고 있어요

18. 저어요

저었어요

저을 거예요

젓고 있어요

Section III - Comprehension

19.

밥 짓는 것은 전혀 어렵지 않아요. 오늘 아침에 저도 밥을 지었어요. 먼저 쌀을 씻어야 돼요. 쌀을 씻기 위해서 물을 부으세요. 물을 부은 다음에 손으로 저으세요. 쌀을 다 씻었으면 그 물만 버리세요. 쌀에 다시 깨끗한 물을 부어서 밥솥에 넣으세요. 그리고 취사 버튼을 <u>누르세요</u>. 그러면 끝이에요. <u>쉽지 않아요?</u>

Section IV - Dictation

20. 감기 다 나았어요?

= Did you recover completely from your cold?

21. 신발을 벗어 주세요.

= Please take your shoes off.

22. 그 문장에 밑줄 그었어요.

= I underlined the sentence.

Lesson 30

Section I - Vocabulary, Part 1

1. toilet; bathroom

2. outdoors, outside

3. indoors

4. head of the office

5. teacher's office

6. office

7. beauty parlor; hairdresser's place

8. hospital room, patient's room

9. meeting room, conference room

10. waiting room

11. practice room, practice place

12. classroom

13. bedroom

14. living room

15. emergency room

16. kitchen (except for the one at home)

17. operating room, operating theater

18. classroom, lecture room (usually in university)

19. break room, resting room, lounge

20. school infirmary

21. principal's office; head teacher's office

22. video arcade

23. smoking room

Section II - Vocabulary, Part 2

24.

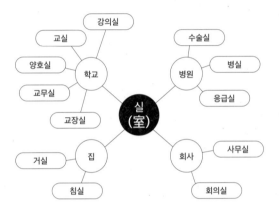

Section III - Dictation

25. 지금 화장실에 누구 있어요?

= Is there anyone in the bathroom now?

26. 침실에 거울이 두 개 있어요.

= There are two mirrors in the bedroom.

27. 사무실에서 이상한 냄새가 나요.

= It smells weird/bad in the office.